RELATIONSHIP MURDERERS

Surviving the Silent Assassins

KEVIN ANTHONY STONE

Table of Contents

Preface

In the intricate tapestry of human connections, relationships can blossom into beautiful unions that bring joy, love, and growth or descend into a dismal demise. At times, it seems as though these relationships are murdered, their life force snuffed out by the toxic presence of ego, disrespect, selfishness, and disloyalty.

In this book, aptly titled "Relationship Murderers," we explore these destructive forces that plague our most intimate connections. We delve deep into the intricate workings of the human psyche, shedding light on the dark corners where egos run unchecked, disrespect festers, selfishness roams free, and loyalty becomes a distant memory

Through careful analysis and introspection, we unravel the mysteries behind these relationship murderers, revealing the havoc they wreak and their profound impact on our emotional well-being.

We examine the origins of ego and its insidious intrusion into our interactions, dismantling the delicate foundations we tirelessly build.

Furthermore, we bravely confront the harsh realities of disrespect, dissecting its various manifestations and uncovering its devastating consequences on the delicate fabric of relationships. We face the brutal truth that selfishness can poison the once-pure intentions of individuals, transforming acts of love into calculated maneuvers for personal gain.

Moreover, we examine the heart-wrenching betrayal of disloyalty, understanding the pain it inflicts and the fractures it creates in our dear bonds. In pursuing personal desires, loyalties are shattered, trust is destroyed, and relationships are left lifeless, mere shells of what they once were.

In this book, we don't shy away from the uncomfortable truths within ourselves and our relationships.

We offer a mirror for self-reflection, inviting readers to confront their inner demons and recognize their potential to nurture or dismantle the connections they hold dear.

However, it is not all despair and hopelessness. Within these pages, we also provide guidance, insights, and practical strategies to help navigate the treacherous waters of ego, disrespect, selfishness, and disloyalty. Through self-awareness, communication, empathy, and the transformative power of forgiveness, we can mend the wounds, rebuild the trust, and resurrect the relationships that these murderers have taken.

May this book serve as a guiding light and a wake-up call for those who find themselves entangled in the clutches of ego, disrespect, selfishness, and disloyalty? Let us embark on this journey together as we uncover the depths of these relationship murderers in search of the healing, growth, and love we all deserve.

INTRODUCTION

Relationships are the building blocks of our lives. They provide love, support, and companionship and play a fundamental role in shaping our identity and sense of belonging. But all too often, these precious bonds are shattered by the insidious presence of ego, disrespect, selfishness, and disloyalty.

In this book, "Relationship Murderers: Ego, Disrespect, Selfishness, and Disloyalty," we delve into the destructive forces that erode the foundation of relationships, causing irreversible damage and heartache. We explore the nature of these relationship murderers and their impact on our personal and professional lives.

Ego, like a poison, can infiltrate even the most vital relationships. It breeds arrogance, selfishness, and a need for control, pushing aside empathy and understanding. Disrespect erodes trust and mutual respect, leaving scars that may never heal.

Greed, fueled by a lack of consideration for others, can tear apart even the most profound connections. And disloyalty, the ultimate betrayal, fractures the bonds of trust and loyalty that hold relationships together.

Through personal anecdotes, psychological insights, and practical advice, we aim to shed light on these relationship murderers and empower readers to recognize their presence in their own lives, as well as in the lives of others. By understanding the dynamics at play and adopting strategies for prevention and repair, we can navigate the treacherous waters of ego, disrespect, selfishness, and disloyalty and salvage or strengthen our most dear relationships.

This book is not a condemnation of human nature but a call to self-awareness and personal growth. By confronting these relationship murderers head-on, we open the door to possibilities for healing, forgiveness, and transformation.

Together, let us embark on a journey to restore harmony, kindness, and loyalty to the relationships that mean the most to us.

So, whether you are struggling in your relationships, witnessing the erosion of connections around you, or simply seeking insight into the complexities of human interaction, "Relationship Murderers: Ego, Disrespect, Selfishness, and Disloyalty" offers a roadmap for navigating the turbulent waters of relationships and emerging more assertive on the other side.

Join us as we uncover the truth behind these silent killers and explore the path toward healthier, more fulfilling connections. It is time to reclaim our relationships from ego, disrespect, selfishness, and disloyalty and create a world where love, kindness, and loyalty reign supreme.

CHAPTER 1

Understanding the Foundations of Relationships

In this chapter, we will delve into the significance of relationships in our lives. We will explore how healthy relationships contribute to our overall well-being and happiness. By understanding the value that relationships hold, we can gain a fresh perspective on their true importance and the devastating impact that their breakdown can have.

1.2 The Definition of Ego and its Impact on Relationships

The ego is an intrinsic part of the human psyche, often driving our actions and influencing our relationship behavior. In this section, we will explore the concept of ego and how it plays a crucial role in shaping the dynamics of relationships.

By gaining a deeper understanding of our egos and how they intersect with our relationships, we can begin to recognize the patterns and behaviors that contribute to their downfall.

1.3 Dissecting Disrespectful Behaviors in Relationships

Respect forms the bedrock upon which healthy relationships are built. Unfortunately, disrespect can erode these foundations and lead to irreparable damage. In this chapter, we will dissect the various forms of disrespect that can permeate relationships, from subtle insensitivity to outright disregard. By recognizing and addressing disrespectful behaviors, we can work towards creating a more respectful and nurturing environment in our relationships.

1.4 The Negative Impact of Selfishness on Relationships

Selfishness is a toxic trait that can slowly poison relationships. In this section, we will explore the destructive nature of selfishness and how it can undermine trust and connection in relationships. Through self-reflection and understanding, we can learn to let go of our selfish tendencies and foster a more selfless approach that nourishes and strengthens our bonds.

1.5 The Betrayal of Disloyalty in Relationships

Loyalty is the essence of a solid and lasting relationship, but when loyalty is broken, the consequences can be devastating. In this chapter, we will delve into the impact of disloyalty and betrayal in relationships – from infidelity to broken promises. By examining the root causes, we can gain insight into how to cultivate and preserve

loyalty and how to rebuild trust after it has been
shattered.

By understanding the foundations of relationships,
including the role of ego, disrespect, selfishness,
and disloyalty, we can confront the relationship
murderers head-on. It is through this understanding
and self-reflection that we can begin to nurture
healthier, more fulfilling connections with our loved
ones, reviving and rejuvenating our relationships for
the better.

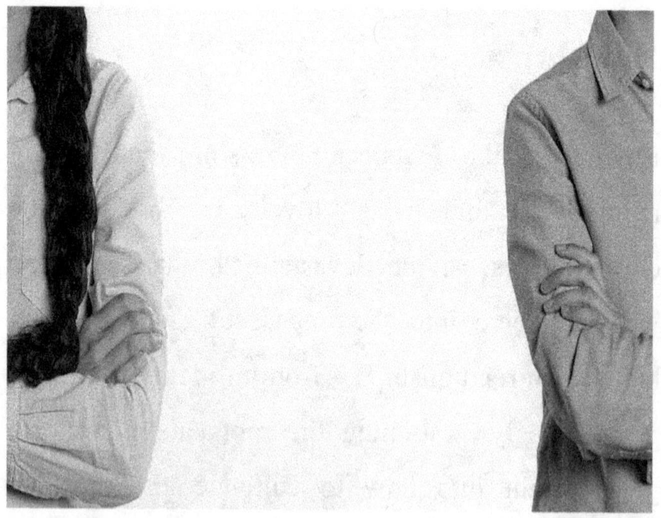

CHAPTER 2

1.1 The Importance of Healthy Relationships

A complex web of relationships weaves our lives together. From our familial connections to our friendships, romantic partnerships, and professional affiliations, relationships form the foundation of our existence. They bring meaning, fulfillment, and happiness to our lives and give us a sense of belonging and support.

1.1.1 Defining Relationships and Their Impac

Relationships encompass a broad spectrum of connections we have with other individuals. They are not limited to romantic partnerships but also include our relationships with friends, family members, colleagues, mentors, and acquaintances. Each relationship contributes to our overall well-being and has the potential to shape our thoughts, emotions, and actions.

The impact of relationships is profound. Healthy relationships have a profound positive effect on various aspects of our lives. They can boost our self-esteem, enhance our mental and emotional well-being, and promote personal growth and development. In contrast, toxic or unhealthy relationships can have devastating consequences on our mental health, self-worth, and overall happiness.

1.1.2 The Benefits of Healthy Relationship

Healthy relationships offer many benefits that enrich our lives in countless ways. They provide emotional support, allowing us to share our joys, sorrows, and challenges with someone who truly understands and cares. A robust support system not only helps us navigate difficult times but also enhances our resilience and coping mechanisms.

Furthermore, healthy relationships foster a sense of belonging and connectedness.

They create a safe space to be our authentic selves, where we are accepted and valued for who we are. This acceptance nurtures our sense of identity and self-confidence, reinforcing the belief that we are worthy of love and belonging.

Moreover, healthy relationships encourage personal growth and self-improvement. They inspire us to become better versions of ourselves by providing constructive feedback, enabling us to embrace new experiences, and challenging us to overcome obstacles. The support, encouragement, and motivation we receive from our loved ones push us to reach our full potential and achieve our goals.

Healthy relationships also contribute to our physical health. Research has shown that individuals in supportive relationships experience lower stress levels, reduced risk of developing mental health disorders, lowered blood pressure, and improved cardiovascular health.

The emotional and physiological support provided by healthy relationships can play a significant role in promoting our overall well-being.

In conclusion, the importance of healthy relationships cannot be overstated. They provide emotional support, a sense of belonging, personal growth, and even physical health benefits. By fostering and nurturing these relationships, we can create a solid foundation for a fulfilling and meaningful life.

1.2 The Role of Ego in Relationships

In relationships, the ego often looms as a silent assassin, lurking in the shadows and ready to strike. Understanding the role of the ego is critical to unraveling the intricate dynamics that can either nurture or destroy our connections with others.

The ego, in psychological terms, refers to the part of our identity that is centered around our sense of self-importance, self-worth, and self-image.

It is the voice within us that seeks validation, recognition, and control. In relationships, the ego can manifest itself in various ways, often leading to conflicts, misunderstandings, and deterioration of individual bonds.

One aspect of the ego's role in relationships is its tendency to prioritize personal needs, desires, and ambitions above the needs of others. When the ego takes control, it often fuels selfishness and self-centered behavior. Individuals driven by their ego will prioritize their wants and aspirations without considering the impact they may have on their partner or the relationship as a whole. This self-serving attitude can create an unbalanced and toxic environment where one person's ego dominates over the needs and well-being of both parties.

Additionally, the ego can contribute to a sense of competition and superiority within relationships. It fuels the need for power and control, leading to a constant power struggle between individuals.

Rather than seeking harmony and collaboration, the ego seeks dominance and superiority, undermining trust, respect, and equality between partners. In such cases, instead of working together as a team, individuals become locked in a battle for control, each trying to assert their ego-driven agenda.

Furthermore, the ego is strongly tied to our self-worth and self-image. When the ego feels threatened, it can lead to defensiveness, aggression, and the inability to handle criticism or conflicts constructively. That can hinder effective communication and problem-solving within relationships as individuals become more concerned with protecting their egos rather than finding common ground and resolving issues.

To foster healthy relationships, it is crucial to recognize and manage the role of the ego. It involves cultivating self-awareness and self-reflection, understanding our ego-driven patterns and tendencies, and consciously working towards a more balanced and compassionate approach.

By prioritizing empathy, understanding, and the well-being of both individuals, we can begin to tame the ego's destructive tendencies and create a foundation of respect, trust, and harmony within our relationships.

In the following chapters, we will explore practical strategies and tools to navigate the complexities of the ego, promoting healthier and more fulfilling relationships. We will delve into the impact of disrespect, selfishness, and disloyalty as we continue our journey toward a deeper understanding of the critical ingredients that contribute to the life and death of relationships.

1.3 Recognizing Disrespectful Behaviors

Respect is the backbone of all successful and fulfilling relationships. It involves treating others with dignity, honoring their boundaries, and valuing their perspectives. However, there are times when disrespectful behaviors creep into our interactions, slowly tearing apart the fabric of our relationships. In this chapter, we will explore various disrespectful behaviors and learn how to recognize them to preserve and enhance the quality of our connections with others.

1.3.1 Verbal Disrespect: Words that wound

- Insults, name-calling, and derogatory language
- Dismissive or belittling remarks
- Mockery and sarcasm

1.3.2 Emotional Disregard: Ignoring feelings and needs

- Dismissing or invalidating emotions
- Ignoring or neglecting the needs of others
- Emotional manipulation and gaslighting

1.3.3 Lack of Boundaries: Crossing the Line

- Intrusion into personal space or privacy
- Disregarding personal boundaries and consent
- Violating trust and confidentiality

1.3.4 Disregarding Opinions and Perspectives

- Dismissing or devaluing someone's ideas or beliefs
- Interrupting, talking over, or dominating conversations
- Disregarding diverse perspectives and experiences

1.3.5 Non-Verbal Disrespect: Actions speak volumes

- Rude gestures or body language
- Eye-rolling, scoffing, or dismissive looks
- Passive-aggressive behavior and silent treatment

By familiarizing ourselves with these various manifestations of disrespect, we become empowered to address them in our relationships. By identifying disrespectful behaviors, we can proactively promote respect, open communication, and harmonious coexistence. As we embark on this journey, let us strive to create and nurture relationships that are built on a foundation of mutual respect and understanding.

1.4 The Negative Impact of Selfishness on Relationships

Selfishness, prioritizing one's own needs and desires above those of others, can be a relationship killer. The presence of selfishness can erode trust, breed resentment, and create an imbalance in power dynamics within relationships. In this chapter, we will explore the negative impact of selfishness and its detrimental effects on the health and longevity of relationships.

1.4.1 Understanding the Nature of Selfishness

- Defining selfishness and its manifestations in relationships
- Exploring the underlying motivations behind selfish behaviors

1.4.2 Recognizing Selfish Behaviors

- Identifying common selfish behaviors in relationships
- Understanding the consequences of these behaviors on the other person

1.4.3 The Erosion of Trust and Intimacy

- How selfishness undermines trust and intimacy in relationships
- The role of communication breakdown and emotional disconnection

1.4.4 Resentment and Discontent

- The development of resentment in relationships marred by selfishness
- The impact of resentment on overall relationship satisfaction

1.4.5 Imbalance of Power and Control

- The link between selfishness and power dynamics within relationships

- Exploring the effects of imbalance on the well-being of both partners.

By understanding the negative repercussions of selfishness, we can cultivate self-awareness and work towards healthier, more balanced relationships that thrive on mutual respect and consideration.

1.5 Understanding the Consequences of Disloyalty

Loyalty is the very essence that holds relationships together, providing a sense of security, trust, and commitment. However, when that loyalty is breached, the consequences can be profound and far-reaching. In this chapter, we will delve deep into the repercussions of disloyalty, exploring its multifaceted impact on individuals and their relationships.

1.5.1 Betrayal and Breach of Trust

Disloyalty often manifests as betrayal, resulting in a fundamental breach of trust. When one person breaks the promise of loyalty and fidelity in a relationship, the damage can be immense.

 The betrayed party grapples with hurt, disbelief, and deep emotional pain. Trust, once shattered, becomes a fragile fragment that is not easily mended.

1.5.2 Erosion of Emotional Connection

Disloyalty can cause a gradual erosion of the emotional connection between individuals in a relationship. The bond that was once strong and vibrant weakens as doubt, suspicion, and insecurity creep in. The betrayed individual may find it challenging to fully trust and open up, fearing that history may repeat itself. The disloyal party, too, may experience guilt and remorse, further straining the emotional fabric of the relationship.

1.5.3 Damage to Self-Esteem and Self-Worth

For the betrayed individual, disloyalty can have a devastating impact on their self-esteem and self-worth. They may question their worthiness, blaming themselves for their partner's actions.

They may feel inadequate, unlovable, and unworthy of being treated with loyalty and respect. Rebuilding one's self-esteem after such a blow requires time, healing, and often external support.

1.5.4 Distrust and Fear of Future Betrayal

Disloyalty leaves a lingering sense of distrust, planting seeds of doubt in the fertile ground of the relationship. The betrayed individual may find it challenging to trust not only their partner but also future partners and potential relationships. The fear of being betrayed again can lead to a guardedness and an unwillingness to fully invest emotionally.

1.5.5 Potential Relationship Breakdown

The consequences of disloyalty can push a relationship to the brink of collapse. Relationships foundation of trust upon which are created crumbles, leaving both parties struggling to salvage what remains.

The road to recovery is long and arduous, requiring sincere effort, understanding, and a genuine desire to rebuild what was lost.

In this chapter, we will delve into these consequences to shed light on how disloyalty can impact individuals and their relationships. By understanding these repercussions, we can navigate the complexities of loyalty and make conscious choices to foster resilience and trust in our connections with others.

CHAPTER 3

2.1 Ego: The Silent Killer of Relationships

In relationships, the ego often acts as a silent killer, lurking in the shadows and ready to strike. Understanding the role of the ego is crucial to preserving and nurturing healthy connections.

The ego can be described as the self-centered part of our identity, driven by our desires, insecurities, and need for validation. It is the voice in our head that constantly seeks to assert itself, protect its self-image, and maintain a sense of superiority.

2.2 Ego-based Behaviors

Ego-based behaviors in relationships often stem from a deep-rooted fear of vulnerability and an obsession with control. These behaviors can manifest in various ways, including:

1. Need for Power and Control: The ego seeks to dominate others, often leading to power struggles, manipulation, and a disregard for the autonomy and agency of the other person.

2. Defensiveness and Blame: The ego is quick to defend itself and deflect responsibility, often blaming others instead of taking accountability for its actions.

3. Lack of Empathy: The ego is primarily concerned with its own needs and desires, making it difficult to empathize with the feelings and experiences of others.

4. Constant Need for Validation: The ego craves constant validation and approval, seeking external sources of proof to maintain its self-worth.

2.3 The Impact of Ego on Relationships

The pervasive influence of ego in relationships can have detrimental effects, leading to conflicts, emotional distancing, and eventual breakdown. Here are some of the critical impacts of ego:

1. Communication Breakdown: Ego-driven behaviors hinder effective communication, as the focus shifts from understanding and connecting to asserting dominance and defending one's position.

2. Lack of Trust: Ego creates an atmosphere of competition and mistrust, eroding the foundation of trust necessary for healthy relationships.

3. Emotional Strain: The ego's need for control and power can create emotional strain, leading to resentment, anger, and disconnection

4. Stifled Growth: Ego-based behaviors restrict personal and relational growth, as the focus remains on protecting one's self-image rather than nurturing the collective development of the relationship.

2.4 Overcoming the Grip of Ego

To overcome the destructive impact of ego, it is essential to cultivate self-awareness, humility, and compassion. Here are some strategies for managing ego in relationships:

1. Reflect on Behavior: Take a step back and reflect on how your ego influences your actions and relationship perceptions. Recognize your ego-driven tendencies and their impact on your connections.

2. Practice Empathy and Active Listening: Cultivate empathy by actively listening and seeking to understand the perspectives and emotions of others. Put yourself in their shoes to foster deeper connection and understanding.

3. Foster Open Communication:

Encourage open and honest communication in your relationships, creating a safe space for vulnerability and transparency.

4. Release the Need for Control: Let go

of the need to control others and outcomes. Embrace the idea that true strength lies in vulnerability and healthy interdependence.

Remember, relationships thrive when ego takes a backseat and genuine connection and understanding take center stage. By acknowledging and addressing the role of ego, we can nurture healthier and more fulfilling relationships.

2.1.1 Defining Ego in Relationships

In relationships, the ego can be described as an individual's self-image or self-identity. It encompasses their beliefs, attitudes, and behaviors that revolve around self-importance and self-centeredness.

The ego in relationships can manifest in various ways. It is the part of us that seeks validation, recognition, and control. It often prioritizes our own needs, desires, and wants over those of others. The ego can inflate our sense of self, leading us to believe that our opinions and perspectives are always correct.

Moreover, the ego often thrives on comparison and competition. It tends to view relationships as a battleground of power and superiority. It can make us defensive, stubborn, and unwilling to compromise. The ego drives us to protect our self-image, sometimes at the cost of damaging our connections with others.

It is important to note that having an ego is not inherently harmful. It is a natural part of being human and helps us establish identity and individuality. However, when the ego becomes destructive and overrides empathy, understanding, and compassion in relationships, it can have detrimental effects.

Understanding the role of the ego in relationships is crucial as it allows us to recognize its influence and work towards maintaining a healthy balance between our own needs and the needs of others. It requires self-awareness, humility, and a willingness to let go of the need for constant affirmation and control. By cultivating a more selfless and compassionate relationship approach, we can create a more harmonious and fulfilling connection with others.

2.1.2 How Ego Damages Communication and Connection

The ego, with its self-centered focus, can inflict significant damage on communication and connection within relationships. Its presence can hinder effective and meaningful communication, leading to misunderstandings, conflicts, and, ultimately, a breakdown in individual relationships.

Here are some ways in which the ego damages communication and relationships:

1. Defensive Attitude: The ego often causes individuals to become defensive when their beliefs, opinions, or actions are challenged. Instead of listening and understanding the perspectives of others, the ego drives them to protect their self-image. This defensiveness creates a barrier to open and honest communication.

2. Lack of Empathy: Ego-centric individuals prioritize their needs, desires, and opinions above others. This self-centeredness makes it difficult for them to truly empathize and understand the emotions and experiences of their partners or loved ones. Without empathy, there is a lack of deep connection and understanding in relationships.

3. Need for Control: Ego-driven individuals often have a strong need for control and dominance. They want to be in charge, make decisions, and

have their way. This desire for control can lead to power struggles and stifle the free flow of communication. It hampers the ability to collaborate, compromise, and work together as equals.

4. Ineffective Listening: When the ego takes over, individuals tend to filter information through their own beliefs, biases, and judgments. They may selectively listen, only paying attention to what aligns with their viewpoints and disregarding or dismissing alternative perspectives. This selective listening prevents proper understanding and hinders meaningful dialogue.

5. Blame Game: Ego-driven individuals often struggle to take responsibility for their mistakes or shortcomings. Instead, they may blame others or external circumstances to protect their ego and avoid feeling inferior. The blame game creates a toxic environment where conflicts escalate, trust is eroded, and connection is severed.

6. Need for Validation: The ego thrives on external validation and approval. Individuals driven by ego often seek constant praise, recognition, and admiration. This constant need for validation can make them insecure and overly sensitive to criticism. It can create an environment where open and honest communication becomes difficult, as individuals fear judgment and rejection.

To overcome the damaging impact of ego on communication and connection, individuals need to practice self-awareness, compassion, and humility. By recognizing and taming their ego, individuals can foster a healthier and more interconnected relationship built on trust, effective communication, and emotional intimacy.

CRIME SCENE DO NOT ENTER

CHAPTER 4

4.1 Cultivating Healthy Relationship

To cultivate healthy and thriving relationships, it is crucial to overcome our egos. The ego, with its self-centered focus, can often hinder genuine connection and growth within relationships. However, by recognizing the impact of ego and actively working towards its transcendence, we can create a more harmonious and fulfilling relational experience.

3.2 Cultivating Self-Awareness

The first step in overcoming ego is developing self-awareness. It involves a deeper understanding of our thoughts, emotions, and behavioral patterns. By becoming more attuned to our ego-driven tendencies, such as the need always to be correct or the desire to control situations, we can start to recognize how they negatively impact our relationships.

4.3 Practicing Empathy and Compassion

Empathy and compassion are potent antidotes to ego-driven behavior. By putting ourselves in the shoes of others, we can gain a better understanding of their perspectives, needs, and emotions. That allows us to let go of our self-centeredness and approach relationships with kindness, compassion, and genuine care.

4.4 Cultivating Open and Honest Communication

Open and honest communication is vital for overcoming ego-driven conflicts and fostering more profound connections. It involves actively listening to others, validating their experiences, and expressing ourselves authentically without judgment. By setting aside our ego's need to be right or to defend ourselves, we create a safe space for open dialogue and mutual understanding.

4.5 Practicing Compromise and Collaboration

Overcoming ego requires a willingness to compromise and collaborate with others. Instead of rigidly clinging to our desires and viewpoints, we must be open to finding mutually beneficial solutions. It involves relinquishing the need to always have our way and embracing the idea of shared decision-making and joint problem-solving.

4.6 Cultivating Gratitude and Appreciation

Gratitude and appreciation are powerful tools in overcoming ego and nurturing positive relationships. By focusing on the qualities, actions, and contributions of others, we shift our attention away from ourselves and towards gratitude for their presence in our lives. Expressing genuine appreciation fosters a more profound sense of connection and strengthens the bonds within the relationship.

4.7 Seeking Growth and Learning Opportunities

Overcoming ego is an ongoing journey of growth and learning. It requires a commitment to personal development, self-reflection, and a willingness to evolve continuously. By embracing this mindset, we create space for humility, curiosity, and the capacity to learn from our mistakes, strengthening our relationships.

In conclusion, overcoming ego for the sake of the relationship is essential for fostering healthy and fulfilling connections. By recognizing the impact of ego, cultivating self-awareness, practicing empathy and compassion, fostering open communication, embracing compromise and collaboration, developing gratitude and appreciation, and seeking growth and learning opportunities, we can transcend ego-driven behaviors and create thriving relationships based on genuine connection, respect, and love.

CHAPTER 5

5.1 Strategies to Reduce Ego-driven Conflicts

Ego-driven conflicts have the potential to wreak havoc on relationships, causing unnecessary tension, misunderstandings, and resentment. The following strategies can help mitigate conflicts that foster a harmonious environment:

1. Developing Self-awareness:

Increasing self-awareness is the first step in reducing ego-driven conflicts. Reflect on your triggers, patterns, and behaviors contributing to conflicts. Recognize when your ego is taking over and be willing to acknowledge your role in the competition.

2. Practicing Empathy: Put yourself in the other person's shoes and try to understand their perspective. Cultivate empathy by actively listening to their concerns, validating their emotions, and showing genuine interest in their point of view.

It helps build a foundation of understanding and reduces the ego's need to be "right."

3. Choosing Collaboration over Competition: Shift your mindset from a competitive perspective to a collaborative one. Instead of trying to prove yourself or win an argument, focus on finding mutually beneficial solutions and compromise. Emphasize teamwork and prioritize the relationship over individual ego-driven desires.

4. Taking Responsibility for Your Actions: Instead of deflecting blame or making excuses, take ownership of your mistakes or shortcomings. Admitting when you're wrong and apologizing shows humility and fosters a sense of accountability. That helps break down ego-driven barriers and opens up the possibility of resolving conflicts more effectively.

5. Practicing Mindfulness: Incorporate mindfulness into your daily life to cultivate a sense of inner calm and awareness.

Mindfulness helps you observe your thoughts and emotions without judgment, allowing you to respond to conflicts with more intention and compassion rather than react impulsively, driven by the ego.

6. Seeking Mediation or Counseling:

In complex situations where ego-driven conflicts persist, seeking the help of a neutral third party such as a mediator or counselor can be beneficial. They can provide guidance, facilitate communication, and help navigate the underlying issues contributing to the conflicts.

By implementing these strategies, individuals can reduce the influence of their egos in conflicts, promote healthier communication, and foster more vigorous, more satisfying relationships. Remember, overcoming ego-driven conflicts takes practice and patience, but the rewards are well worth the effort.

5.2 Understanding Disrespect in Relationships

Disrespect has the power to poison even the strongest of relationships. It is a toxic force that undermines the bonds of trust, undermines communication, and erodes the very foundation on which relationships are built. In this chapter, we will delve into the damaging effects of disrespect and explore ways to address and overcome it.

5.3 The Effects of Disrespect in Relationships

Disrespect creates a hostile and unhealthy atmosphere within relationships, leaving behind a trail of negative consequences. Some of the effects of incivility include:

1. Erodes Trust: When disrespect becomes a recurring pattern in a relationship, trust begins to crumble. Respect is a fundamental aspect of faith, and without it, the foundation becomes weak.

2. Breaks Communication: Disrespectful behavior hinders open and honest communication. It creates a defensive atmosphere where individuals feel unheard and invalidated, leading to a breakdown in effective communication.

3. Damages Self-esteem: Being treated with disrespect can chip away at an individual's self-esteem. Constant belittlement and disregard for their thoughts and feelings can leave them devalued and unworthy.

4. Build Resentment: Persistent disrespect breeds resentment within relationships. Constantly feeling disrespected can create a build-up of

negative emotions, resulting in resentment towards the offending party.

5. Causes Emotional Distance:

Disrespectful behavior creates emotional distance between partners.

When one person consistently engages in disrespectful actions or words, the other person may withdraw emotionally as a coping mechanism to protect themselves.

5.4 Strategies to Address and Overcome Disrespect

It is essential to address the poison of disrespect in relationships through proactive steps toward fostering respect and creating a healthy dynamic. Here are some strategies to consider:

1. Open Communication: Create a safe space for open and honest communication.

Encourage each other to express their thoughts and feelings without fear of judgment or disrespect.

2. Set Boundaries: Establish clear boundaries that define acceptable behavior in the relationship. Communicate these boundaries to ensure that both partners understand and respect them.

3. Practice Empathy: Cultivate empathy towards your partner's feelings and experiences. Try to understand their perspective and validate their emotions.

4. Seek Professional Help: If disrespect persists and becomes ingrained in the relationship, seeking the guidance of a professional therapist or counselor can be beneficial in addressing the underlying issues and fostering a healthier dynamic.

5. Lead by Example: Be mindful of your actions and words, ensuring that you treat your partner respectfully. Lead by example and embody the behavior you wish to see in the relationship.

6. Foster a Culture of Appreciation:

Focus on the positive aspects of your partner and consistently show appreciation for their efforts and contributions. That can help create a more respectful and supportive environment.

By actively reducing disrespect and promoting respect within the relationship, couples can rebuild trust, strengthen communication, and foster a healthier, more fulfilling partnership.

Remember, respect forms the foundation upon which all successful and fulfilling relationships are built.

4.4 Different Manifestations of Disrespect

Disrespect can take many forms within relationships, making it essential to identify these manifestations to address and resolve them effectively. Here are some familiar images of disrespect:

1. Contemptuous behavior: Contempt is

a strong feeling of disregard or disdain towards someone. You can express it through verbal and non-verbal cues such as eye-rolling, sarcasm, mocking, or belittling remarks.

Contemptuous behavior diminishes the other person's worth and undermines their self-esteem.

2. Dismissing opinions and feelings:

Disrespect can be present when one person consistently dismisses or ignores the thoughts, ideas, and emotions of their partner. That can manifest as interrupting, minimizing, or invalidating their feelings, making them feel unimportant or unheard.

3. Lack of boundaries and personal

space: Respecting boundaries is essential in any relationship, and the absence of this respect can indicate disrespect. That can include invading personal space without permission, disregarding requests for alone time, or violating privacy.

4. Withholding information or affection: Keeping important information or emotions from a partner is disrespectful. It demonstrates a lack of trust, transparency, and emotional availability.

Deliberately withholding love, attention, or intimacy can also be a way to exert power and control over the other person.

5. Public humiliation or embarrassment: Disrespect can occur when one person intentionally humiliates or embarrasses their partner in front of others. That can include making derogatory comments, sharing private or sensitive information without consent, or purposefully embarrassing them in social settings.

6. Disregarding boundaries of consent: Respecting boundaries of support is crucial in a healthy relationship. Disrespect may occur when one person disregards the other's boundaries regarding physical intimacy, emotional disclosure, or any other form of personal consent.

It is important to note that disrespect can manifest in various other ways, and each relationship may have its unique dynamics.

Understanding these manifestations can serve as a starting point for identifying and addressing the issue of disrespect in a relationship.

CHAPTER 6

5.1 The Power of Respect in Building Strong Bonds

Respect is a fundamental pillar of building strong and healthy bonds. It is the cornerstone of every meaningful relationship, fostering trust, appreciation, and mutual understanding.

Respect, at its core, is about valuing and honoring the inherent worth and dignity of others. It involves treating others with kindness, empathy, and consideration, regardless of differences in opinion, background, or beliefs.

5.2 Cultivating Respect in Relationships

Building and maintaining a foundation of respect requires conscious effort and a commitment to ongoing growth. Here are some strategies for cultivating respect in relationships:

1. Active Listening: Truly listening to others without interruption or judgment shows respect for their thoughts and feelings. It demonstrates that you value their perspective and are willing to engage in meaningful dialogue.

2. Open-Mindedness: Embracing an open-minded approach allows for diverse viewpoints and opinions. Respect involves recognizing that everyone has a unique perspective and being willing to consider alternative views.

3. Empathy and Understanding: Putting yourself in someone else's shoes fosters empathy and understanding. Seek to understand their experiences, emotions, and motivations, even if you don't necessarily agree with them.

4. Boundaries and Consent: Respecting boundaries and obtaining consent is crucial in any healthy relationship.

Recognize and honor personal physical and emotional limits, and ensure permission is given willingly and clearly.

5. Communicate Respectfully: Practice respectful communication using kind and considerate language and avoiding insults or derogatory remarks. Choose words carefully and express yourself honestly while prioritizing empathy and sensitivity.

6. Appreciation and Gratitude: Expressing genuine appreciation and gratitude for others strengthens bonds and reinforces respect. Acknowledge their contributions, affirm their value, and show gratitude for their presence in your life.

7. Conflict Resolution: Approach conflicts respectfully by seeking resolutions that honor both parties' perspectives. Avoid personal attacks and instead focus on finding common ground and understanding.

By nurturing a culture of respect within relationships, individuals can build strong bonds based on trust, empathy, and mutual appreciation. The power of care lays the foundation for a harmonious and fulfilling connection with others.

5.3 Communication Strategies to Foster Respect

Respectful communication is crucial in maintaining harmonious and healthy relationships. It involves not only expressing oneself clearly and effectively but also attentively listening to others. Here are some strategies to foster respect through communication:

1. Active Listening: Show genuine interest in the other person's words. Give your undivided attention, maintain eye contact, and refrain from interrupting or formulating responses in your mind while they are speaking. Truly listen to understand their perspective and validate their feelings.

2. Use "I" statements: When expressing your thoughts, feelings, or concerns, use "I" statements to take personal responsibility for your opinions and emotions. Instead of blaming or accusing the other person, express your experiences and needs.

3. Empathy and Understanding: Put yourself in the other person's shoes and try to understand their point of view. Show empathy by acknowledging their feelings and validating their experiences, even if you disagree.

4. Respectful Tone and Body Language: Pay attention to your tone of voice and body language, ensuring they convey respect and openness.

 Speak calmly and avoid aggressive or disrespectful gestures. Maintain an open posture and avoid crossing your arms or showing dismissive gestures.

5. Constructive Feedback: When providing feedback or addressing conflicts, choose your words carefully.

Frame your feedback constructively and non-confrontational, focusing on the issue rather than attacking the person. Aim for a collaborative approach to problem-solving.

6. Boundaries and Respectful Disagreements: Establish and communicate clear boundaries to ensure both parties feel respected and heard. If disagreements arise, approach them respectfully, without resorting to personal attacks or belittling the other person's opinions.

7. Appreciation and Encouragement: Show appreciation for the other person's contributions, ideas, and efforts. Offer encouragement and support to boost their self-esteem and foster a positive relationship dynamic.

Remember, effective communication is a continuous process that requires practice and conscious effort. By implementing these strategies, you can enhance respect within your relationships and foster deeper connections with others.

CHAPTER 7

6.1 Setting Boundaries to Address Disrespectful Behavior

Setting boundaries is a crucial aspect of addressing and resolving disrespectful behavior within relationships. Limitations serve as guidelines to communicate to others how we expect to be treated and what behavior is acceptable or unacceptable. They help create a sense of safety, respect, and healthy communication within the relationship.

6.2 Types of Boundaries

Different types of boundaries to address disrespectful behavior:

6.2.1 Personal Boundaries: These boundaries revolve around individual needs, values, and preferences. It involves being aware of personal limits and communicating them to others.

6.2.2 Emotional Boundaries: Emotional boundaries limit how others interact with your emotions and feelings. That includes defining what is acceptable in terms of emotional support and empathy.

6.2.3 Physical Boundaries: Physical boundaries limit the physical space and touch that others can invade. It consists in communicating personal comfort levels and respecting personal space.

6.2.4 Time and Energy Boundaries:

Time and energy boundaries define how you allocate your time and energy. It includes limiting how much time and energy you are willing to invest in certain relationships or activities.

6.3 Communicating and Enforcing Boundaries

To effectively set boundaries and address disrespectful behavior, it is important to communicate them clearly and assertively without aggression or anger. Here are some steps to consider:

6.4 Maintaining and Revisiting Boundaries

Setting boundaries is an ongoing process. It is essential to revisit and adjust limits as needed regularly. Communicate any changes in your borders and continue to enforce them consistently.

Remember, setting boundaries is a powerful tool for addressing and resolving disrespectful behavior. It empowers you to create a healthy and respectful relationship dynamic.

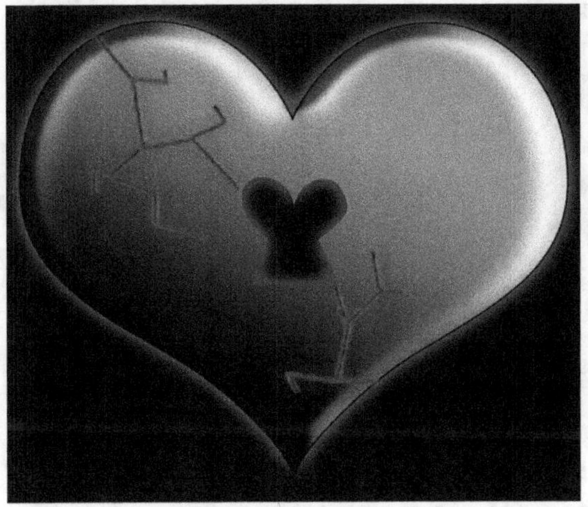

CHAPTER 8

7.1 Selfishness: Destroying the Foundation of Relationships

Selfishness can erode the foundation of a healthy and thriving relationship. When one or both partners prioritize their interests and needs above the relationship's needs, it creates an atmosphere of imbalance, resentment, and disconnection. Selfishness destroys the foundation of trust, compromises effective communication, and prevents genuine emotional intimacy.

7.2 The Signs of Selfishness in Relationships

Recognizing the signs of selfishness is crucial in addressing and resolving this destructive behavior. Some common symptoms include:

1. Lack of consideration: Selfish individuals often disregard the feelings and needs of their partner.

They make decisions without considering how they may impact their partner or the relationship as a whole.

2. Constant need for validation: Selfish individuals may constantly seek confirmation and attention, putting their ego and needs above the emotional well-being of their partner.

3. Frequent disregard for boundaries: Selfish individuals may have little respect for their partner's boundaries and may consistently push for their desires and demands without regard for the feelings or comfort of their partner.

4. Unwillingness to compromise:

Selfish individuals struggle with compromise and may be unwilling to meet their partner halfway or find mutually beneficial solutions in conflict resolution.

5. Lack of empathy: Selfish individuals

often struggle to empathize with their partner's emotions and experiences, as they primarily focus on their wants and needs.

7.3 Overcoming Selfishness for the Sake of the Relationship

Overcoming selfishness requires self-awareness, willingness to change, and active efforts to prioritize the relationship's needs. Here are some strategies to work towards overcoming selfish tendencies:

1. Cultivate empathy: Practice putting yourself in your partner's shoes and make an effort to understand and empathize with their perspective genuinely.

2. Practice active listening: Pay attention to your partner's needs, concerns, and desires.

Listen actively and validate their feelings, even if it means prioritizing their needs over your own in certain situations.

3. Communicate openly and honestly: Foster an environment of open and honest communication where both partners feel comfortable expressing their needs and concerns. Be willing to have difficult conversations and work together to find compromises and solutions.

4. Prioritize the relationship: Make a conscious effort to prioritize the well-being and happiness of the relationship over individual wants and desires. That may require making sacrifices, compromises, and adjustments for the greater good of the partnership.

5. Seek professional help if needed: If selfishness continues to be a persistent issue in the relationship, consider seeking the guidance of a couples therapist or counselor who can help facilitate healthier communication patterns and address underlying issues.

By actively working towards selflessness and prioritizing the relationship's needs, it is possible to rebuild the foundation and create a stronger and more fulfilling bond.

CHAPTER 9

7,1 Understanding Selfishness and its Motivations

Selfishness in relationships can stem from various motivations. It is essential to understand these underlying factors to address and proactively deal with selfish behavior.

Some common motivations for selfishness include:

1. Fear and insecurity: Selfishness can arise from a fear of being vulnerable or hurt. Some individuals may prioritize their own needs and desires as a defense mechanism to protect themselves from potential pain or rejection.

2. Lack of empathy: Some people may struggle to consider the feelings and needs of others genuinely. They may have difficulty empathizing with their partner and instead focus solely on their wants and needs.

3. Unresolved past experiences: Past experiences, such as trauma or previous relationships, can shape one's behavior in current relationships. If someone has experienced neglect or betrayal, they may develop a self-focused mindset as a way of self-protection.

4. Conditioning and societal influences: Society often encourages individualism and self-centeredness. People may adopt selfish behaviors due to societal norms prioritizing personal success and gratification over the collective well-being of a relationship.

7.3 Reflection and Self-Awareness

Understanding the motivations behind selfishness requires deep reflection and self-awareness. Individuals must examine their behaviors, beliefs, and patterns within relationships. By exploring their causes, individuals can begin to address and challenge their selfish tendencies.

This process may involve seeking therapy, engaging in self-reflection exercises, or having open and honest conversations with their partner. Self-awareness allows individuals to recognize when they act selfishly and take steps toward change.

7.4 Cultivating Empathy and Open Communication

To address selfishness in relationships, cultivating empathy and improving communication is essential. Considering and understanding your partner's perspective fosters empathy and allows for a more balanced and respectful dynamic.

Open communication is crucial in addressing selfish behavior. Expressing your concerns, needs, and feelings assertively but without blame can help create a safe space for dialogue and understanding between partners.

7.5 Seeking Support and Growth

Addressing selfishness in relationships may require professional support, such as couples therapy or individual counseling. A trained therapist can guide individuals and couples in exploring their patterns of desire and provide strategies for developing healthier relationship dynamics.

You can overcome Selfishness through self-reflection, increased empathy, open communication, and a commitment to growth. By understanding the motivations behind selfish behavior and actively working towards change, individuals can rebuild trust, foster connection, and create a foundation of respect and mutual consideration in their relationships.

CHAPTER 10

9.1. The Long-Term Impact of Selfishness on Relationship Dynamics

Selfishness can have profound and long-lasting effects on relationship dynamics. It creates a toxic cycle perpetuating negativity, resentment, and emotional distance. The impact of narcissism can manifest in various ways, including:

1. Deterioration of Trust: Selfishness erodes trust between partners. When one person consistently prioritizes their own needs without considering the impact on their partner, it undermines the sense of reliability and support in the relationship.

2. Communication Breakdown: Selfishness often leads to poor communication. The focus on personal desires makes it challenging to engage in open, honest, and empathetic dialogue.

This communication breakdown can lead to misunderstandings, arguments, and further distancing between partners.

3. Emotional Distance: Selfishness creates emotional distance between partners. When one person consistently puts themselves first, it leaves their partner feeling neglected, unvalued, and emotionally disconnected. Over time, this can lead to emotional detachment and a lack of intimacy.

4. Resentment and Conflict: Selfishness breeds resentment within the relationship. The partner who feels consistently disregarded or taken advantage of may begin to harbor deep-seated resentment, which can lead to frequent conflicts and contribute to an unhealthy dynamic.

5. Relationship Dissatisfaction: The long-term impact of selfishness is often relationship

dissatisfaction. When one or both partners prioritize their needs ahead of the relationship, it diminishes overall satisfaction and happiness.

The relationship becomes unfulfilling, and the partners may start considering alternatives.

9.2 Breaking the Cycle of Selfishness

Every partner must be willing to address the long-term impact of selfishness on relationship dynamics to break the cycle and cultivate more empathy. You can achieve them through:

1. Self-reflection: Each partner should reflect on their actions and motivations to understand their selfish behavior patterns. This self-awareness is the first step towards change.

2. Open and Honest Communication: Partners should have open and honest conversations about the impact of selfishness on the relationship. Sharing feelings and concerns can help foster understanding and motivate change.

3. Setting Boundaries: Establishing clear boundaries and expectations can help mitigate selfish behavior. Both partners should have a mutual understanding of what is acceptable and what is not.

4. Practicing Empathy and Compromise: Couples should actively practice empathy and strive to understand each other's perspectives and needs. Finding compromises that meet both partners' needs can foster a more balanced and fulfilling relationship.

5. Seeking Professional Help: In cases where selfishness is deeply ingrained in the relationship dynamics, seeking the guidance of a couples therapist or relationship counselor can be beneficial. They can provide advice, support, and

techniques to navigate the challenges and promote healthier dynamics.

Breaking the cycle of selfishness requires effort, patience, and a willingness to prioritize the relationship's well-being over individual desires. By addressing the long-term impact of greed, partners can work towards rebuilding trust, improving communication, and fostering a more loving, supportive, and fulfilling relationship.

9.3 Developing Empathy and Selflessness

Empathy and selflessness are crucial to maintaining healthy and fulfilling relationships. They involve putting oneself in the other person's shoes and prioritizing their needs and feelings alongside our own.

9.2 Strategies for Developing Empathy

Developing empathy requires practice and intention. Some strategies to cultivate compassion include actively listening to others, seeking to understand their perspectives, and being open to different viewpoints. It also involves being aware of and managing our own biases and judgments.

9.3 Cultivating Selflessness

Being selfless means placing the welfare of others before our own. It involves acts of kindness, generosity, and consideration. Cultivating selflessness can be achieved by consciously choosing to prioritize the needs and happiness of others, practicing empathy, and reframing our mindset towards a more selfless perspective.

9.4 Nurturing a Balanced Relationship

Achieving a healthy balance between empathy and selflessness is vital. It is essential to care for others without neglecting our well-being and boundaries. Communicating openly, setting healthy boundaries, and practicing self-care are crucial to maintaining this balance.

By developing empathy and selflessness, individuals can foster deeper connections, understanding, and harmony within their relationships.

CHAPTER 11

10.1 Techniques to Cultivate Selflessness in Relationships

One of the foundational techniques to cultivate selflessness in relationships is practicing active listening. That means fully engaging in the conversation, giving your full attention to the speaker, and seeking to understand their perspective without interrupting or judgment. By being present and attentive, you are showing respect and valuing the other person's thoughts and feelings.

10.2 Practicing Empathy

Empathy is the ability to understand and share the feelings of another person. To cultivate selflessness, it is essential to practice empathy. Put yourself in the other person's shoes and try to see things from their perspective.

You can do that by actively listening, asking open-ended questions, and genuinely seeking to understand their emotions and experiences.

10.3 Considering the Needs of Others

Selflessness involves considering the needs and desires of others. Ask your partner or loved ones about their needs and actively work towards meeting them. That can include compromising, making sacrifices, and making decisions that prioritize the well-being and happiness of the other person.

10.4 Acts of Kindness and Service

Engaging in acts of kindness and service is a practical way to cultivate selflessness in relationships. Look for opportunities to help, support, or surprise your partner or loved ones without expecting anything in return.

Acts of kindness can range from small gestures like making them breakfast in bed to more prominent acts like helping them with a project or taking care of their responsibilities when they are overwhelmed.

10.5 Practicing Gratitude

Gratitude is closely linked to selflessness. Take the time to express gratitude for the people in your life and how they contribute to your happiness and well-being. Cultivating a grateful mindset helps shift the focus from oneself to acknowledging and appreciating the efforts and contributions of others.

By implementing these techniques and making a conscious effort to prioritize the needs and happiness of others, you can cultivate selflessness in your relationships and create a foundation of love, understanding, and deep connection.

CHAPTER 12

11.1 Disloyalty the Ultimate Betrayal

Disloyalty in relationships is considered the ultimate betrayal, as it undermines the trust and foundation of the relationship. It involves the breaking of commitments, secrets, or fidelity and can have devastating effects on both partners.

11.2 Recognizing Signs of Disloyalty

It is crucial to recognize signs of disloyalty to address and confront the issue. These signs may include secretive behavior, sudden changes in routine or behavior, unexplained absences, and inconsistency in communication or emotional availability.

11.3 Healing and Rebuilding Trust

Rebuilding trust after experiencing disloyalty is a challenging process that requires open communication, honesty, and commitment from both partners. It involves acknowledging the hurt and betrayal, expressing emotions, working towards forgiveness, and establishing new boundaries and expectations.

11.4 Seeking Professional Help

In some cases, seeking the help of a professional therapist or counselor may be necessary to navigate the complex emotions and challenges of addressing disloyalty in a relationship. A trained professional can guide and support both partners in rebuilding trust and healing from the betrayal.

11.5 Defining Disloyalty and its Forms

Disloyalty in relationships refers to a breach of trust and commitment, where one or both partners fail to uphold the loyalty and faithfulness expected. It manifests in various forms, including:

1. Infidelity: This disloyalty involves engaging in sexual or romantic activities outside the committed relationship, betraying the trust and exclusivity expected within the partnership.

2. Emotional Infidelity: Emotional disloyalty occurs when one partner develops an intimate emotional connection with someone outside the relationship, sharing personal thoughts, feelings, and desires that should be reserved for the committed partner.

3. Lack of Support: Disloyalty can also manifest through a lack of support and consideration for the partner's needs and goals.

That includes not being there for them during challenging times, not providing emotional or practical support, and failing to prioritize their well-being.

4. Breaking Promises: Disloyalty can involve repeatedly breaking promises or commitments within the relationship, undermining trust and stability.

5. Withholding Trust: A lack of trust and suspicion towards the partner, without valid reasons or evidence, can erode loyalty within the relationship, leading to feelings of betrayal and insecurity.

It's important to note that the severity of disloyalty can vary, and its impact on the relationship depends on individual circumstances and the willingness of both partners to work towards rebuilding trust and repairing the breach.

11.6 The Devastating Effects of Disloyalty

Disloyalty in relationships can have devastating effects that can profoundly impact both individuals and the relationship itself. The betrayal of trust and commitment can create a sense of brokenness, hurt, and insecurity. The consequences of disloyalty may include:

1. Loss of trust: Disloyalty shatters the foundation of faith in a relationship. The betrayed partner may find it difficult to trust their partner again, leading to heightened suspicion and doubt in future interactions.

2. Emotional pain: The betrayed partner often experiences intense emotional pain, including feelings of betrayal, deceit, and heartbreak. This pain can lead to emotional distress, depression, and a loss of self-esteem.

3. Communication breakdown: Disloyalty can severely damage communication within a relationship. Open and honest communication becomes challenging when there is a lack of trust and fear of further betrayal.

4. Relationship strain: Disloyalty places significant pressure on the relationship. It may lead to arguments, resentment, and a gradual breakdown of the emotional connection. In some cases, it can result in the end of the relationship altogether.

5. Self-doubt: The betrayed partner may question their worth and blame themselves for the disloyalty. This self-doubt can affect their overall well-being and make it challenging to rebuild confidence.

6. Difficulty moving forward:

Rebuilding the relationship after disloyalty requires immense effort from both partners. It takes time, patience, and a commitment to healing.

However, the memories of the betrayal may linger, making it challenging to move forward and fully recover.

It is essential to address the devastating effects of disloyalty through open communication, seeking professional help, and a willingness to rebuild trust and commitment.

TRUST
Takes years to build,
seconds to break and
forever to repair.

CHAPTER 13

12.1 The Importance of Rebuilding Trust

After experiencing betrayal and a breach of trust, rebuilding trust becomes crucial for the survival and healing of the relationship. Faith is the foundation of any healthy relationship, and without it, the connection and intimacy suffer.

12.2 Acknowledging the Betrayal

The first step in rebuilding trust is acknowledging the betrayal and its impact. Both the betrayer and the betrayed need to openly and honestly acknowledge the hurt, pain, and consequences caused by the betrayal. This acknowledgment is essential for starting the healing process.

12.3 Taking Responsibility and Showing Remorse

The betrayer must take full responsibility for their actions and show genuine remorse for the pain they caused. That involves understanding the impact of their behavior, empathizing with the betrayed partner, and expressing sincere apologies.

12.4 Open and Honest Communication

Rebuilding trust requires open and honest communication between both partners. The betrayed partner needs to express their feelings, concerns, and boundaries, while the betrayer must listen attentively, validate those feelings, and respond with empathy and understanding.

12.5 Consistency and Transparency

Consistency and transparency are vital elements in rebuilding trust. The betrayer needs to demonstrate consistent, trustworthy behavior over time.

It includes being reliable, following through on commitments, and being transparent about their actions and whereabouts.

12.6 Patience and Understanding

Rebuilding trust takes time, and both partners need to be patient with the process. The betrayed partner may struggle with trust issues and have moments of doubt or insecurity. The betrayer must offer patience, understanding, and reassurance to help rebuild that trust.

12.7 Seeking Professional Help

In some cases, rebuilding trust after betrayal may require professional help. Couples therapy or counseling can provide a safe and supportive environment for both partners to process their emotions, work through the betrayal, and learn healthy communication and coping skills.

Remember, rebuilding trust after a betrayal is a challenging journey. Still, with commitment, effort, and both partners' willingness to heal, it is possible to restore confidence and rebuild a stronger, more resilient relationship.

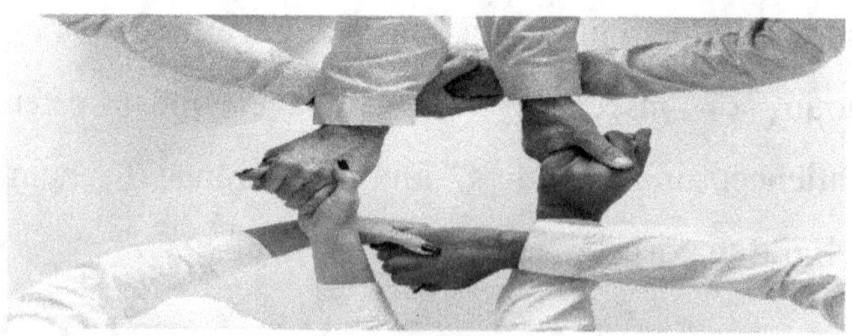

CHAPTER 14

13.1 Understanding the Importance of Commitment and Loyalty

Commitment and loyalty are essential for building and maintaining healthy, strong, and long-lasting relationships. They provide a sense of security, trust, and closeness between partners.

13.2 Techniques to Build Commitment and Loyalty

1. **Open and Honest Communication:** Clear and transparent communication builds commitment and loyalty. It creates a safe space for expressing needs, concerns, and expectations. Encourage open dialogue and active listening to foster understanding and connection.

2. Prioritize Quality Time Together:

Make spending quality time with your partner a priority. Dedicate time for meaningful activities, conversations, and shared experiences. It helps strengthen the bond and fosters a more profound sense of commitment and loyalty.

3. Express Appreciation and Gratitude: Regularly express appreciation and gratitude towards your partner for their contributions, support, and presence. Acknowledge their efforts and let them know they are valued, which promotes a sense of commitment and loyalty.

4. Consistency and Reliability: Be consistent and reliable in your actions and words. Show up for your partner consistently, keep your promises, and be dependable. That builds trust and demonstrates your commitment and loyalty.

5. Practice Empathy and Understanding: Cultivate empathy and understanding towards your partner's emotions, needs, and perspectives. That helps create a compassionate and supportive environment that encourages commitment and loyalty.

6. Collaborative Decision-making: Involve your partner in decision-making processes and value their input. Collaboration fosters a sense of equality, respect, and shared responsibility, strengthening the commitment and loyalty within the relationship.

7. Nurture Individual Growth: Encourage and support each other's personal growth and goals. By nurturing individual development, you create an atmosphere where both partners feel supported, valued, and motivated, further enhancing commitment and loyalty.

8. Seek Professional Help if Needed:

If you are struggling with commitment or loyalty issues, consider seeking the help of a couples therapist or relationship coach. They can provide guidance, support, and tools specific to your situation to help you strengthen and rebuild these aspects of your relationship.

Remember, building commitment and loyalty is an ongoing process that requires dedication, effort, and mutual understanding. By consistently practicing these techniques, you can foster a deep sense of commitment and loyalty that strengthens your relationship.

13.3 Recognizing the Need for Healing

In every relationship, there may come a time when healing and strengthening are necessary. That can be due to conflicts, misunderstandings, trust issues, or other challenges that have caused strain within the relationship.

It is essential to recognize and acknowledge the need for healing to move forward and cultivate a healthier and stronger bond.

13.4 Open and Honest Communication

One of the critical techniques for healing and strengthening relationships is open and honest communication. That involves expressing thoughts, feelings, and concerns respectfully and non-confrontational. It is crucial to actively listen to your partner, allowing them to express themselves without interruption or judgment. By fostering open and honest communication, you create a safe space for both parties to be heard and understood, leading to greater understanding and resolution of conflicts.

13.5 Rebuilding Trust

If trust is broken within the relationship, rebuilding is essential for healing and strengthening the bond.

It requires consistency, transparency, and sincerity from both partners.

Rebuilding trust takes time and effort, and it is essential to be patient and understanding throughout the process. It may involve setting boundaries, following through on commitments, and demonstrating trustworthy behavior. By actively rebuilding trust, you can create a solid foundation for a healthier and more resilient relationship.

13.6 Seeking Professional Help

Sometimes, healing and strengthening a relationship may require the assistance of a professional. A couples therapist or counselor can provide guidance, support, and tools to help navigate challenges and facilitate positive change. Seeking professional help does not signify weakness; instead, it shows a commitment to the relationship and a willingness to invest in its growth and well-being.

In conclusion, healing and strengthening relationships require recognizing the need for healing, practicing open and honest communication, rebuilding trust, and seeking professional help when needed. With dedication, effort, and mutual commitment, relationships can grow, evolve, and strengthen, leading to greater satisfaction and fulfillment for both partners.

Healing doesn't mean the damage never existed. It means the damage no longer controls our lives.

CHAPTER 15

14.1 Steps towards Healing Wounded Relationships

The first step towards healing a wounded relationship is to acknowledge the hurt and pain that both parties have experienced. That involves being open and honest about your feelings and allowing yourself to express the emotions pent up genuinely.

14.2 Communicate and Listen

Open and effective communication is crucial in the healing process. Take the time to have an open and honest conversation with the other person, expressing your feelings and concerns while listening to their perspective. Practice active listening and strive to understand their point of view without interrupting or judging.

14.3 Apology and Forgiveness

Apologizing for any wrongdoing or hurt you may have caused is an essential step toward healing. Take responsibility for your actions and express genuine remorse. Equally important is the act of forgiveness. Decide to let go of any resentment or grudges and be willing to forgive the other person for any pain they may have caused you. Remember, forgiveness is a process that takes time and effort.

Remember, healing a wounded relationship takes time, effort, and a willingness from both parties to participate in the process actively. Be patient, kind, and compassionate towards each other as you navigate the road to healing and strengthening your relationship.

CHAPTER 16

15.1 Cultivating Emotional Intelligence in Relationships

Emotional intelligence refers to the ability to recognize, understand, and manage our own emotions and the emotions of others. It plays a crucial role in building and maintaining healthy relationships.

15.2 Developing Self-Awareness

One of the critical aspects of emotional intelligence is self-awareness. That involves being able to identify and understand our own emotions, as well as the triggers and patterns that affect our behavior in relationships. Developing self-awareness allows us to recognize better how our emotions impact our interactions with others.

15.3 Practicing Empathy

Empathy is the ability to understand and share the feelings of another person. It involves putting ourselves in their shoes and viewing the situation from their perspective. By practicing empathy, we can deepen our connection with our partners and respond to their emotions with understanding and compassion.

15.4 Managing Conflict and Resolving Disagreements

Conflicts are inevitable in any relationship, but emotional intelligence can help us navigate them constructively and respectfully. By recognizing and managing our emotions during disputes, we can communicate openly and honestly, seek compromise, and work towards finding mutually satisfactory solutions.

15.6 Practicing Emotional Regulation

Emotional regulation is the ability to control and manage our emotions. That is important in relationships, as it allows us to respond to situations with emotional balance and avoid impulsive or harmful reactions. Emotional regulation involves techniques such as deep breathing, mindfulness, and self-care to help us maintain dynamic equilibrium.

By cultivating emotional intelligence in relationships, we can foster deeper connections, enhance understanding and empathy, and navigate conflicts and challenges more healthily and constructively.

15.7 Promoting Open Communication and Vulnerability

Open communication and vulnerability are essential elements in building and maintaining solid bonds in relationships.

When partners can express themselves honestly and authentically, it fosters a sense of trust, understanding, and connectedness. Here are some strategies to promote open communication and vulnerability:

1. Create a safe and non-judgmental space:

Establish an environment where both partners feel comfortable sharing their thoughts, feelings, and concerns without fear of judgment or criticism. You can do that by actively listening, showing empathy, and refraining from interrupting or becoming defensive.

2. Practice active listening:

When your partner is sharing something with you, give them your full attention. Focus on understanding their perspective rather than formulating your response. Reflect on what you've heard to ensure you've understood correctly, and ask clarifying questions if needed.

3. Express yourself honestly: Be open and honest about your thoughts, feelings, and needs.

Avoid holding back or sugarcoating your emotions, leading to misunderstandings and distance. Authentically expressing yourself allows your partner to understand you better and for both of you to work through challenges together.

4. Be vulnerable: Share your fears, insecurities, and vulnerabilities with your partner. That helps to deepen emotional intimacy and creates an opportunity for your partner to provide support and reassurance. Remember, vulnerability is not a sign of weakness but rather a sign of strength and trust.

5. Encourage open dialogue: Create regular opportunities for open discussion, such as dedicated "check-in" time or date nights. These intentional conversations allow both partners to openly discuss concerns, reinforce their commitment, and ensure they agree.

By actively promoting open communication and vulnerability, couples can create a strong foundation for their relationship, fostering trust, understanding, and intimacy.

CHAPTER 17

16.1 Sustaining Healthy Relationships

Sustaining healthy relationships is crucial for long-term happiness and fulfillment. It involves nurturing and maintaining the connection between partners by fostering open communication, showing appreciation, prioritizing quality time, and adapting to changes together. By investing time and effort into sustaining a healthy relationship, individuals can create a strong foundation for a fulfilling and lasting partnership.

16.2 Nurturing the Relationship despite Challenges

In any relationship, challenges and difficulties are inevitable. However, it is essential to nurture the relationship despite these challenges to maintain a healthy and fulfilling connection. Here are some strategies to help you promote your relationship despite the challenges:

16.3 Fostering Mutual Respect and Trust

Mutual respect and trust are the core components of a strong and healthy relationship. They create a foundation of safety, openness, and support, essential for long-term happiness and fulfillment. Here are some helpful strategies for fostering mutual respect and trust:

1. **Communication:** Open and honest communication is crucial to building trust. Create a safe space for both partners to express their thoughts, feelings, and concerns without fear of judgment or criticism. Active listening and empathetic responses help validate each other's experiences and perspectives.

2. **Consistency:** Consistency in words and actions is essential for building trust. Ensure your

actions align with your comments and follow through on your commitments. This consistency ensures your reliability and shows that you can be trusted.

3. Transparency: Be open and transparent with each other. Share important information and be willing to be vulnerable. Keeping secrets or hiding important details erodes trust, so it's essential to be honest and upfront.

4. Boundaries: Respect each other's boundaries and communicate them. Understanding and honoring each other's limits fosters a sense of safety and trust. It shows that you value and respect each other's autonomy.

5. Dependability: Be dependable in your actions and obligations. Show up for each other and fulfill your promises. Consistently demonstrating dependability builds trust over time.

6.   Forgiveness: Mistakes and misunderstandings are inevitable in any relationship. Practicing forgiveness allows for the growth and healing of the relationship. It's essential to let go of past grievances and move forward.

7. Support: Show support and encouragement for each other's goals, dreams, and aspirations. Being each other's cheerleader helps foster trust and demonstrates that you have each other's best interests at heart.

Remember, building mutual respect and trust takes time and effort from both partners. It requires open communication, consistency, transparency, respect for boundaries, and a willingness to forgive and support each other. With these strategies, you can nurture a relationship based on trust and respect, creating a solid foundation for a lasting bond.

16.4 Balancing Individual Needs in a Relationship

In a healthy relationship, it is crucial to find a balance between meeting your individual needs and the needs of your partner. Striving for this balance helps to promote equality, understanding, and satisfaction in the relationship.

To achieve this balance, it is essential to communicate openly and honestly about your needs and expectations. Both partners should express their desires and concerns, allowing for a mutual understanding of needs.

Additionally, it is essential to show empathy and respect towards your partner's needs. That means acknowledging and validating their individuality and understanding that their needs may differ from your own.

Finding the right balance also requires compromise. It involves making sacrifices and adjustments to accommodate each other's needs without compromising your values and boundaries.

Remember, balancing individual needs is an ongoing process that requires active effort from both partners. Regular check-ins and discussions about needs and expectations can help maintain this balance throughout the relationship.

By prioritizing the needs of both individuals and working together to find common ground, you can foster a healthy and fulfilling relationship built on mutual respect and understanding.

16.5 The Role of Forgiveness in Relationship Maintenance

Forgiveness plays a vital role in maintaining healthy and thriving relationships. It allows individuals to let go of resentment, hurt, or anger that their partner's actions may have caused. It is not about condoning or forgetting what happened but rather about releasing the negative emotions attached to the event.

When we forgive, we create space for healing, growth, and the possibility of rebuilding trust. It is important to note that forgiveness is a process that takes time and effort. Here are some steps to foster forgiveness in a relationship:

1. Acknowledge and validate your emotions: Allow yourself to feel and recognize the pain or hurt caused by your partner's actions. Avoid suppressing or denying your feelings, which may hinder the forgiveness process.

2. Understand the situation: Seek to understand your partner's perspective and the circumstances that led to their actions. That doesn't justify their behavior but can provide insight into their motives or struggles.

3. Express your feelings and concerns: Communicate openly with your

partner about how their actions affected you. It is crucial to express your emotions calmly and non-confrontationally, allowing space for them to understand the impact of their actions on you.

4. Seek empathy and remorse:

Forgiveness requires a genuine sense of guilt from the offending partner.

They should take responsibility for their actions and demonstrate compassion toward your feelings.

5. Establish boundaries: Forgiveness does

not mean accepting repeated hurtful behavior. Set boundaries with your partner about what is acceptable, and communicate the consequences of crossing those boundaries.

6. Commit to the forgiveness

process: Forgiveness is an ongoing process that

requires commitment from both partners. It may involve seeking professional help like counseling or therapy to navigate complex emotions and promote healing.

7. Let go and move forward: Once forgiveness is granted, it is essential to consciously let go of the resentment and negative emotions attached to the situation. Remember that forgiveness is not for the offender's benefit but your emotional well-being.

Forgiveness can be a powerful tool in maintaining and strengthening relationships.

It fosters an environment of empathy, understanding, and growth. However, it is essential to remember that forgiveness is a personal choice, and it may not always be possible or appropriate in all situations.

16.6 Infidelity and Forgiveness in Relationships

Infidelity can have a devastating impact on a relationship, causing pain, betrayal, and a loss of trust. However, forgiveness can play a significant role in the healing and rebuilding process after infidelity.

Forgiveness does not mean forgetting or condoning the actions of the unfaithful partner. Instead, it is a process of letting go of anger, resentment, and the desire for revenge. It involves acknowledging the hurt and pain caused by the infidelity and making a conscious decision to move forward.

Forgiveness in the context of infidelity is a complex and individual journey.

It requires open communication, honesty, and a commitment to rebuilding trust. Both partners must be willing to participate actively in the healing process and make necessary changes to prevent further infidelity.

Counseling or therapy can be beneficial for couples working through the aftermath of infidelity. It provides a safe space to explore emotions, rebuild trust, and develop strategies for moving forward.

It is important to note that forgiveness does not guarantee the relationship's survival. Rebuilding trust takes time, effort, and a genuine commitment to change. Both partners need to assess the underlying issues that may have contributed to the infidelity and work towards addressing them.

Ultimately, the decision to forgive after infidelity is a personal one. It requires introspection, empathy, and a willingness to embark on a journey of healing and growth.

With patience, understanding, and a shared commitment, it is possible to rebuild trust and create a stronger, more resilient relationship after infidelity.

16.7 The consequences of committing Infidelity in a long-lasting relationship

Committing infidelity in a long-lasting relationship can have significant consequences. Not only does it cause emotional pain and turmoil for the partner who has been betrayed, but it also undermines the foundation of trust and intimacy within the relationship. The consequences of infidelity can include:

1. Emotional Trauma: The partner who has been cheated on often experiences a profound sense of betrayal, heartbreak, and emotional trauma. They may struggle with low self-worth, self-blame, anger, and mistrust.

2. Breakdown of Trust: Infidelity shatters the essential trust for a healthy relationship. It can be challenging to rebuild trust after infidelity, and it may take a significant amount of time and effort from both partners to regain confidence and establish a sense of security again.

3. Communication Challenges: Committing infidelity often leads to breakdowns in communication within the relationship. The betrayed partner may have difficulty expressing

their emotions and concerns, while the cheating partner may struggle with guilt and shame. Effective communication becomes essential to work through these challenges and rebuild the relationship.

4. Intimacy Issues: Infidelity can have a profound impact on the physical and emotional intimacy between partners. The betrayed partner may struggle to feel safe and vulnerable again, hindering the ability to rebuild intimacy.

The cheating partner may also experience guilt, impacting their ability to be fully present and engaged within the relationship.

5. Relationship Dissolution: In some cases, the consequences of infidelity can be so severe that the relationship becomes irreparable. The betrayed partner may decide to end the relationship due to the breach of trust and inability to move forward. However, with sincere effort and commitment from both partners, it is possible to rebuild a relationship after infidelity.

It is important to note that every relationship is unique, and the consequences of infidelity may vary depending on the individuals involved. Seeking professional help, such as couple's therapy, can provide guidance and support for navigating the aftermath of an affair and working towards healing and growth.

CHAPTER 18

17.1 The causes of infidelity

Infidelity in a relationship is a complex issue that can stem from various underlying causes. Understanding these causes can provide insight into the reasons behind infidelity and help navigate its challenges. Some common causes of infidelity include:

1. Lack of Emotional Fulfillment:

When one or both partners feel emotionally

disconnected or unsatisfied in the relationship, they may seek emotional intimacy outside of it.

2. Lack of Communication: Poor communication and unresolved issues can create a gap in the relationship, leading individuals to seek validation and connection elsewhere.

3. Sexual Dissatisfaction: Dissatisfaction with sexual intimacy can lead individuals to look for sexual fulfillment outside of their relationship.

4. Relationship Problems: Issues such as constant conflict, unresolved resentments, or a lack of commitment can weaken the bond between partners and make them more susceptible to infidelity.

5. Emotional or Physical Neglect: A partner's consistent neglect of emotional or physical needs can lead individuals to seek validation and attention elsewhere.

6. Opportunity and Temptation:

Opportunities for infidelity occur when traveling for work or spending time in environments with potential partners and can increase the likelihood of straying.

7. Personal Factors: Individual factors,

such as low self-esteem, thrill-seeking behavior, or a history of infidelity, can contribute to the decision to cheat.

These causes are not meant to excuse or justify infidelity but to shed light on the underlying dynamics that can contribute to its occurrence. Couples need to address these root causes and work towards healing and strengthening their relationship to prevent future instances of infidelity.

17.2 The Gap between Infidelity and Lies

A significant gap between the truth and the deceitful behavior of the unfaithful partner often accompanies infidelity. This gap can stem from various factors contributing to the breakdown of trust and the willingness to deceive.

One factor that can contribute to this gap is a breakdown in communication within the relationship. When partners fail to openly and honestly communicate their needs, desires, and concerns, it can create a breeding ground for secrets and dishonesty.

Issues left unaddressed or unresolved may lead one partner to seek emotional or physical fulfillment outside the relationship, leading to infidelity.

Another factor is a lack of emotional satisfaction or fulfillment. When one partner feels emotionally neglected or unsatisfied, they may seek validation, intimacy, or companionship elsewhere. That can lead to an affair that provides the emotional connection they are missing in their current relationship.

In some cases, individuals may engage in infidelity due to personal issues or insecurities. Low self-esteem, a fear of intimacy, or a desire for novelty and excitement can drive someone to seek validation or thrills outside the relationship. These factors can create a gap between their actions and the truth they present to their partner.

Additionally, external circumstances can contribute to the gap between infidelity and lies.

Life stresses, such as financial difficulties, work pressures, or family problems, can strain a relationship and make one partner more susceptible to seeking comfort or escape outside of it.

Ultimately, the gap between infidelity and lies can be a result of multiple factors intertwined within the dynamics of the relationship. Addressing these underlying causes is essential in rebuilding trust, fostering open communication, and working towards healing and recovery.

17.3 Confession and Forgiveness in Infidelity Occurrence

Confession and forgiveness in the occurrence of infidelity can be a profoundly challenging and emotionally intense process. Here's a vivid description of what it entails:

The moment of confession hangs heavy in the air as the unfaithful partner gathers the courage to reveal their betrayal.

With fear, guilt, and remorse, they find themselves standing before their partner, heart pounding and hands trembling. The weight of their secret threatens to suffocate them, but they know that honesty is the only way forward.

As they stumble over their words, the unfaithful partner unravels their actions, laying bare the extent of their infidelity. With each painful detail uttered, they witness the impact of their betrayal reflected in their partner's eyes – shock, disbelief, and the raw hurt of betrayal. Tears fall freely as both parties confront the harsh reality of the situation.

In this vulnerable moment, the betrayed partner struggles to process the overwhelming emotions. They feel anger, sadness, and a profound sense of betrayal. Questions whirl in their mind, demanding answers, seeking understanding, and hoping for reassurance.

As the confession unfolds, a delicate dance between confession and forgiveness begins.

Amidst the pain and turmoil, the betrayed partner weighs the possibilities of forgiveness, wrestling with conflicting emotions. They question the authenticity of their partner's remorse, grappling with trust shattered to its core.

Forgiveness becomes a daunting and complex journey. It requires both partners to navigate a treacherous path, acknowledging the betrayed partner's pain while allowing the unfaithful partner to take responsibility for their actions. Honest conversations, raw and vulnerable, become the foundation for rebuilding trust – an arduous process that demands patience, open communication, and unwavering commitment.

The betrayed partner faces a tumultuous internal struggle, oscillating between anger and the desire to salvage the relationship. They must assess the sincerity of their partner's remorse, seeking signs of actual change and ensuring that the confession is not merely a hollow act of remorse to ease their guilt.

Genuine remorse, demonstrated through consistent actions and transparency, becomes the lifeline for forgiveness. The unfaithful partner must demonstrate their commitment to healing the wounds they inflicted. They willingly subject themselves to opening up their lives, sharing passwords, and allowing their partner to access the previously undisclosed aspects of their existence.

Forgiveness does not happen overnight. It evolves slowly as the betrayed partner grapples with their pain, learning to trust again and navigating the emotional rollercoaster of healing. Small steps forward are celebrated, and setbacks are met with patience and understanding.

In this delicate dance of confession and forgiveness, both partners must confront their vulnerabilities, face brutal truths, and commit to rebuilding a foundation of trust. It is a flawed and imperfect journey, but through open communication, empathy, and shared determination, healing becomes a possibility – a tender blooming amid the ruins of infidelity.

17.4 Caught in the Act and Forgiveness

Discovering your partner's infidelity can be a devastating experience, especially when you catch them in the act. However, forgiveness can still play a role in the healing process.

The scene is etched in your mind as you walk through the front door, unaware of the betrayal that awaits you. Suddenly, you hear hushed whispers and unfamiliar voices coming from the bedroom. Your heart races as you approach, your instincts telling you something is amiss. You push open the door, and your worst fears are confirmed. The sight before you feels like a punch to the gut. Your partner, caught in the act of infidelity, freezes with guilt and shock written all over their face.

At that moment, raw emotions surge through you - anger, hurt, and disbelief - all colliding in a tornado of emotions. It feels as if your world has shattered into a million irreparable pieces. Forgiveness may be the last thing on your mind.

However, in the aftermath of the initial shock, you may begin to contemplate the possibility of forgiveness. It isn't an easy path to walk, and the road is fraught with pain and uncertainty. Questions tumble through your mind - Can I ever trust them again? Are they genuinely remorseful? Can our relationship survive this betrayal?

Forgiveness, in this context, is not about condoning the actions or minimizing the pain caused. It is a personal journey of healing, both for yourself and your relationship. It involves confronting the painful truth, acknowledging the betrayal, and deciding whether forgiveness is a path you're willing to consider.

Forgiveness, in this context, may involve open and honest communication between you and your partner. They may express deep remorse, taking responsibility for their actions and promising to make amends. It may also involve seeking professional help, such as therapy or counseling, to navigate the complex emotions and rebuild trust.

However, forgiveness is not a guaranteed outcome. It is a deeply personal decision that only you can make. It requires time, self-reflection, and careful consideration of whether rebuilding the relationship is the best choice for your emotional well-being.

Caught in the act may seem like an unattainable concept of forgiveness. But in some cases, with sincere remorse and a shared commitment to therapy and healing, forgiveness can become a possibility. It may not instantly erase the pain, but it allows for the potential of growth, rebuilding, and, ultimately, finding a way forward, whether together or separately.

17.5 Can the act be erased from memory?

The question of whether you can erase infidelity from memory is a complex and challenging one. While it is not possible to completely erase a memory, significantly one as impactful as infidelity, the healing process can help to mitigate its painful effects.

Imagine a couple grappling with the aftermath of infidelity, seeking to move forward and rebuild their relationship. The betrayed partner, plagued by intrusive thoughts and vivid images of the betrayal, desires nothing more than to erase those painful memories. They yearn for a clean slate, a mind free from the burden of the past.

In their pursuit of healing, they embark on a journey of open communication, therapy, and emotional support. Together, they confront the painful details of the infidelity, acknowledging the hurt and betrayal. Through heartfelt conversations, they address the underlying issues that led to this breach of trust.

The betrayed partner, with time and effort, begins to find solace in knowing that the infidelity does not define their entire relationship. They focus on the positive aspects, the shared memories, and the growth they have experienced together. They consciously work towards creating new, positive memories to overwrite the negative ones.

Professional help, such as couples therapy, can guide you in navigating the path to healing. Through this process, they learn coping mechanisms to manage triggers and intrusive thoughts. They develop strategies to communicate their needs, fears, and insecurities in a safe environment.

As time goes by and the relationship strengthens, the memory of the infidelity may lose some of its power. While it may never be erased, it becomes less intrusive and disruptive. Trust slowly rebuilds, and the couple cultivates a renewed sense of security and connection.

It is important to note that everyone's journey of healing is unique, and not all relationships can or should overcome the impact of infidelity. Sometimes, even with forgiveness, the memory of the act remains a reminder of boundaries and the need for ongoing work in the relationship.

In summary, you cannot completely erase infidelity from memory, but through the healing process, individuals and couples can find ways to cope, heal, and move forward. The goal is not to erase the memory but to mitigate its impact and create a new foundation of trust and growth.

17.6 Conclusion on infidelity

Infidelity is a profoundly complex issue that can have profound effects on a relationship. Throughout this chapter, we have explored various causes and aspects related to infidelity, including the gap between infidelity and lies, confession and forgiveness, being caught in the act, and the lingering impact on memory.

The gap between infidelity and lies highlights the disparity between the truth and the deceptive behavior of the unfaithful partner. It can stem from underlying issues within the relationship, such as lack of communication, emotional disconnection, or dissatisfaction.

Confession and forgiveness play vital roles in the healing process when infidelity occurs. The moment of confession is laden with tension and emotional weight as the unfaithful partner must confront their actions and face the consequences. The journey towards forgiveness is a difficult one, requiring open communication, empathy, and a willingness to rebuild trust.

Being caught in the act is a devastating experience for both the betrayed partner and the unfaithful partner. It shatters trust and further emphasizes the depth of betrayal. However, even in such a profound breach, forgiveness can still be sought and achieved with dedicated effort and commitment.

When it comes to the memory of infidelity, it cannot be erased. The impact of the affair reverberates, leaving a mark on the betrayed partner's psyche. However, through therapy, self-reflection, and a genuine healing process, it is possible to lessen the intensity of the memory and strive for restoration within the relationship.

In conclusion, infidelity is a complex issue that requires deep introspection, open communication, and a commitment to rebuilding trust and repairing the relationship. While the journey towards healing may be difficult, a relationship can recover and grow more robust if both partners are willing to put in the necessary effort and work through the underlying issues that led to infidelity in the first place.

CONCLUSION

In the journey through the chapters of this book, we have delved into the intricate dynamics of relationships, focusing on critical elements such as communication, trust, individual needs, forgiveness, and the challenging topic of infidelity.

We have explored how healthy relationships require a delicate balance between meeting individual needs and our partners' needs, emphasizing the importance of open and honest communication. Understanding the role of forgiveness and its significance in maintaining a thriving relationship has been elucidated, particularly in the face of infidelity.

Infidelity, with its devastating consequences, has been examined in-depth, acknowledging the profound pain and loss of trust that it can cause. Whether it be the gap between infidelity and lies, the process of confession and forgiveness, or the impact of being caught in the act, we have confronted the challenges head-on.

While it is impossible to erase the memory of infidelity, it is vital to recognize that healing and growth are possible. Moving forward requires immense effort, open communication, and a shared commitment to rebuilding trust.

As we conclude this book, may it serve as a guide to navigating the complex terrain of relationships, providing insights, tools, and understanding to cultivate and sustain healthy, fulfilling partnerships? Remember, relationships are a continuous journey, and with dedication, resilience, and love, they can flourish even in the face of adversity.

Acknowledgments

I want to express my sincere gratitude to all those who have supported and contributed to the creation of this book. I am deeply thankful for the unwavering support and encouragement from my family, friends, and loved ones throughout this journey.

References

1. "The Seven Principles for Making Marriage Work" by John M. Gottman and Nan Silver

2. "Attached: The New Science of Adult Attachment and How It Can Help You Find - and Keep - Love" by Amir Levine and Rachel Heller

3. "The Relationship Cure: A 5-Step Guide to Strengthening Your Marriage, Family, and Friendships" by John M. Gottman

4. "Boundaries: When to Say Yes, How to Say No to Take Control of Your Life" by Henry Cloud and John Townsend

5. "The Four Agreements: A Practical Guide to Personal Freedom" by Don Miguel Ruiz

6 The Four Agreements" by Don Miguel Ruiz

7. The Dance of Anger: A Woman's Guide to Changing the Patterns of Intimate Relationships" by Harriet Lerner -

8. The State of Affairs: Rethinking Infidelity" by Esther Perel

9 The Narcissism Epidemic: Living in the Age of Entitlement" by Jean M. Twenge and W. Keith Campbell